Made possible through a grant from
The Fremont Area Community
Foundation

Fremont Area
community foundation

CHILDREN'S ILLUSTRATORS

TONY DITERLIZZI

Sheila Griffin Llanas

ABDO Publishing Company

visit us at
www.abdopublishing.com

Printed in the United States of America, North Mankato, Minnesota.
102011
012012

 PRINTED ON RECYCLED PAPER

Cover Photo: courtesy Tony DiTerlizzi
Interior Photos: courtesy Angela DiTerlizzi p. 9; courtesy Carole DiTerlizzi p. 11;
      courtesy Tony DiTerlizzi pp. 5, 10, 13; courtesy Jim Gaynor p. 15; Getty Images pp. 19, 21
      Reprinted with the permission of Simon & Schuster Books for Young Readers, an imprint of Simon & Schuster Children's Publishing Division from *Ted* by Tony DiTerlizzi. Copyright © 2001 Tony DiTerlizzi. pp. 6–7
      Reprinted with the permission of Simon & Schuster Books for Young Readers, an imprint of Simon & Schuster Children's Publishing Division from *The Spider and the Fly* by Tony DiTerlizzi. Based on the cautionary tale by Mary Howitt. Cover illustration copyright © 2002 Tony DiTerlizzi. p. 17
      Reprinted with the permission of Simon & Schuster Books for Young Readers, an imprint of Simon & Schuster Children's Publishing Division from *The Spiderwick Chronicles, Book 1: The Field Guide* by Tony DiTerlizzi and Holly Black. Copyright © 2003 Tony DiTerlizzi and Holly Black. p. 18

Series Coordinator: BreAnn Rumsch / Editors: Megan M. Gunderson, BreAnn Rumsch
Art Direction: Neil Klinepier

Library of Congress Cataloging-in-Publication Data

Llanas, Sheila Griffin, 1958-
  Tony DiTerlizzi / Sheila Griffin Llanas.
      p. cm. -- (Children's illustrators)
  Includes index.
  ISBN 978-1-61783-245-1
  1. DiTerlizzi, Tony--Juvenile literature. 2. Illustrators--United States--Biography--Juvenile literature. I. DiTerlizzi, Tony. II. Title.
  NC975.5.D58L59 2012
  741.6'42--dc23
  [B]
                                        2011027843

CONTENTS

IMAGINATIVE ARTIST

Tony DiTerlizzi first became famous as a fantasy artist. Some fans love his characters and figures from the role-playing game Dungeons & Dragons. Others adore the world he later created for The Spiderwick Chronicles chapter book series.

For both games and books, DiTerlizzi lets his imagination run wild. He draws strange and mysterious creatures, such as kelpies, nixies, knockers, griffins, and gargoyles!

DiTerlizzi's creative art inspires the imaginations of others. Many young people send him fan letters and their own art inspired by his creations. DiTerlizzi is honored by these tributes to his work and often posts them on his Web site.

On a normal day, DiTerlizzi runs errands, reads his mail, and answers phone calls in the morning. After lunch, he heads to work in his art studio.

There, a *Raiders of the Lost Ark* movie poster hangs on one wall. A 1980s Pac-Man arcade game stands in the corner. DiTerlizzi's bookshelves are packed with books, and art supplies and toys cover his desk. In his studio, DiTerlizzi writes, draws, and paints. He works hard to bring his ideas to life. Lucky for his fans, DiTerlizzi works a lot!

Tony DiTerlizzi puts much of himself into his art. "I really try to create from my heart and soul so that it is true to me," he once said.

A Love of Fantasy

Tony DiTerlizzi was born in Los Angeles, California, on September 6, 1969. He grew up in Jupiter, Florida, with his younger **siblings**, Adam and Jennifer. Tony's father, Anthony, worked as an engineer. He designed aircraft engines. His mother, Carole, stayed home with the children.

The DiTerlizzis were an artistic family that owned lots of books. Tony's mother often read aloud to her children. Tony's favorite authors

were Dr. Seuss and Shel Silverstein. He also loved the classic fairy tales by the Brothers Grimm.

Tony enjoyed listening to these stories. He also used his imagination to make up stories. He brought them to life as drawings of dinosaurs, UFOs, and fantastic creatures. Tony filled sketchbooks with his many creations.

One time, Tony even drew on the walls. His parents were not happy! But then, Tony's father taped butcher paper onto the walls. He said, "Now you can draw on the walls." Tony thought that was awesome!

Tony's childhood experiences helped influence his books later in life. He included his memory of drawing on the walls in Ted.

TONY'S FIELD GUIDE

Though Tony had always loved stories, reading did not come as easily as drawing did. Then Tony's fifth grade teacher, Ray Straussberger, had an idea. He asked Tony to illustrate his book reports for extra credit. Drawing story scenes helped Tony improve his reading skills. He earned better grades too!

Growing up, Tony had wide-ranging interests. He liked *Star Wars*, music by Elton John, and Jim Henson's the Muppets. He enjoyed playing Dungeons & Dragons, too.

Tony also loved nature. In his free time he participated in Boy Scouts, rode his bike, and collected insects. Tony also studied John James Audubon's field guides to birds and flowers.

When Tony was 12, he created his own field guide to fantastic beings. He drew detailed dragons, trolls, ogres, and fairies. He even thought up Latin scientific names for them! Tony kept his field guide for a long time. He never forgot his ideas. One day, they would serve as inspiration for one of his most famous projects.

At a young age, Tony already knew he would one day be an artist. He eventually created and published his well-known *Arthur Spiderwick's Field Guide to the Fantastical World Around You.*

TONY IN WONDERLAND

At South Fork High School in Stuart, Florida, Tony took every art class offered. His art teacher, Mr. Wetzl, challenged Tony to illustrate a classic novel. Tony chose to illustrate *Alice's Adventures in Wonderland* by Lewis Carroll.

Tony's drawings had to add something new to the story. So he carefully studied the book and developed his creative

vision. After months of work, Tony's project impressed his teacher as well as his classmates. This boosted Tony's **confidence** and he began considering children's art as a future career.

Even as a high school student, Tony already demonstrated great skill as an artist.

In 1987, Tony graduated. During the following year, he took classes at the Florida School of the Arts in Palatka. Then he began attending the Art Institute of Fort Lauderdale.

At the Art Institute, he found a book in the library called *A Treasury of the Great Children's Book Illustrators* by Susan E. Meyer. It was filled with the work of artists he admired such as Arthur Rackham and Beatrix Potter. Tony was awestruck by their mastery. He knew he needed to take his craft seriously.

In 1992, Tony graduated with a degree in graphic design. His first job was drawing real estate maps back in Jupiter. But this was not his goal, so Tony began sending his **portfolio** to publishers. Yet, he got no job offers. Tony wondered if he would ever achieve his dream.

In high school, Tony entered many art competitions. Sometimes he won!

DRAWING DRAGONS

During this frustrating time, DiTerlizzi began playing Dungeons & Dragons again with some friends. One day, his friend Mike suggested he could do art for the game. DiTerlizzi's brother and his other friends agreed.

So over the summer, DiTerlizzi drew a few illustrations of monsters. In September, he sent them to Tactical Studies Rules (TSR), the company that published Dungeons & Dragons.

DiTerlizzi waited more than a month to hear from TSR. When a rejection letter came, DiTerlizzi felt crushed. It took courage, but he called TSR's art director, Peggy Cooper. He asked her what was wrong with his artwork.

Cooper told him that TSR needed illustrations of action characters, not monsters. She suggested that DiTerlizzi send new drawings. So DiTerlizzi got back to work. This time Mike said, "Make the characters as cool as the monsters." His advice inspired DiTerlizzi.

In the end, DiTerlizzi's determination paid off! TSR hired him as an illustrator. His work included designing a whole new game world called Planescape. He went on to illustrate for other games too, such as the collectible card game Magic the Gathering.

ELEMENTS OF ART: TEXTURE

Texture is one of the most basic parts of art. Texture is how a piece of art feels or looks like it would feel.

DiTerlizzi uses pencils, pens, and gouache watercolor paints to bring his artwork to life. He draws many detailed lines to create fantastic creatures with realistic textures. These include bark, scales, fur, feathers, and insect wings. The gouache adds texture, too. DiTerlizzi can make the colors look solid or see-through.

HELLO, NEW YORK!

DiTerlizzi continued to draw for TSR for six years. He enjoyed this work, but he still dreamed of becoming a children's book illustrator. During that time, DiTerlizzi remained in Florida. There, he met a woman named Angela DeFrancis. They enjoyed spending time together and soon fell in love. In 1996, the couple moved to New York City, New York.

In the big city, DiTerlizzi looked for work illustrating children's books. Many editors liked his art, but no one made him any job offers. Finally, editor Kevin Lewis showed a stronger interest in DiTerlizzi's art. But he also wondered if DiTerlizzi had any stories to go with his drawings.

DiTerlizzi showed Lewis his story about a boy named Jimmy Zangwow. Jimmy loves MoonPies enough to go to outer space to get them. Lewis liked the story enough to give DiTerlizzi his first book contract.

The colorful *Jimmy Zangwow's Out-of-this-World Moon Pie Adventure* was published in 2000. With that, DiTerlizzi learned he could be a great writer as well as a great artist. This realization changed his life.

At bookstore signings for Jimmy Zangwow, DiTerlizzi handed out real MoonPies to kids who came to see him!

MORE PICTURE BOOKS

Over the next few years, DiTerlizzi kept busy creating picture books. In 2001, DiTerlizzi published his second book, *Ted*. The boy in the story has a busy father, so he invents an imaginary friend named Ted.

DiTerlizzi's third picture book, *The Spider and the Fly*, was published in 2002. It is based on the 1829 **cautionary tale** by poet Mary Howitt. The book features a dainty fly and a bad-guy spider.

Each of DiTerlizzi's books had a **unique** style. He filled *Jimmy Zangwow* with rich, bold colors. Jimmy wears red cowboy boots, a yellow shirt, and blue pants. He meets blue-headed Martians on an orange Mars. He also faces the green Grimble Grinder.

For *Ted*, DiTerlizzi painted scenes in tones of strawberry, pistachio, vanilla, and chocolate. The ice cream-colored book won the **Zena Sutherland Award** in 2002.

DiTerlizzi made all his illustrations for *The Spider and the Fly* black and white. Cool effects make the text glow and ghosts appear see-through! The book was a *New York Times* best seller and earned DiTerlizzi another **Zena Sutherland Award** in 2003.

DiTerlizzi loves to walk outside and take close-up photographs of insects for inspiration. This helped him create his characters for **The Spider and the Fly.**

That same year, DiTerlizzi realized his dream had come true. *The Spider and the Fly* was named a **Caldecott Honor Book**! DiTerlizzi's illustrating career had taken off. So what book would he make next?

SPIDERWICK SENSATION

In 2002, DiTerlizzi moved from New York to Amherst, Massachusetts. His friend Holly Black lived there too. She was also a writer. Black knew about old fairy folklore and helped DiTerlizzi research a project he was planning. DiTerlizzi was going to make a field guide to fairies, trolls, and goblins. *Arthur Spiderwick's Field Guide to the Fantastical World Around You* was inspired by the guide he had created when he was 12.

Black and DiTerlizzi enjoyed working together. As they developed the story of

The Spiderwick Chronicles book series has sold over 7 million copies!

DiTerlizzi and Black (right) *attended the opening of*
the **Spiderwick Chronicles** *movie in 2008.*

Aurthur Spiderwick's fairy field guide, the Spiderwick Chronicles also came to life. In the story, the Grace **siblings** move into their aunt's large Victorian home. There, they discover a secret library and encounter many mysterious creatures.

Black wrote chapters while DiTerlizzi drew pictures. To create the images, DiTerlizzi started with pencil. Then with old-fashioned dip pens and ink, he went over the pencil lines. For color images, he added watercolor paints. His pug dog, Goblin, even modeled for a few creatures!

The first book, *The Spiderwick Chronicles: The Field Guide*, came out in 2003. It was a huge success! The popular fantasy inspired young readers everywhere. Other books in the series soon followed. And in 2007, DiTerlizzi and Black started a **sequel** series called Beyond the Spiderwick Chronicles.

REAL-LIFE MAGIC

In spite of the success of his Spiderwick books, DiTerlizzi kept working hard. In 2006, his alphabet book *G is for One Gzonk!* came out under the name Tiny DiTerlooney. And his next novel, *Kenny and the Dragon*, came out in 2008. It is about a young rabbit who befriends a dragon named Grahame.

During 2009 and 2010, DiTerlizzi's Adventure of Meno series was published. He **collaborated** on the four picture books with his wife, Angela. DiTerlizzi also published *The Search for WondLa* in 2010. This futuristic fairy tale novel is the first in a **trilogy** about a girl named Eva Nine.

Today, DiTerlizzi spends the winter months in Jupiter, Florida. DiTerlizzi also enjoys spending his free time with his family. He likes collecting art and antiques with Angela and exploring nature with his daughter, Sophia.

DiTerlizzi sketched a scene from **The Search for WondLa** *for young readers at the book's launch party in New York.*

DiTerlizzi's life seems as magical as his art. He once said in an interview, "I keep waiting for my mom to wake me up." But he is not dreaming. In creating fantasy art, DiTerlizzi also created a fantastic real life.

GLOSSARY

Caldecott Honor Book - a runner-up to the Caldecott Medal. The Caldecott Medal is an award the American Library Association gives to the artist who illustrated the year's best picture book.

cautionary tale - a story that offers a warning.

collaborate - to work with another person or group in order to do something or reach a goal.

confidence - faith in oneself and one's powers.

portfolio - a selection of work, especially of drawings, paintings, or photographs. It may be presented to show one's skill as an artist.

sequel - a book, movie, or other work that continues the story begun in a preceding one.

sibling - a brother or a sister.

trilogy - a series of three novels, movies, or other works that are closely related and involve the same characters or themes.

unique - being the only one of its kind.

Zena Sutherland Award - an award given by students to three picture books each year. The categories are best text, best illustrations, and best overall.

WEB SITES

To learn more about Tony DiTerlizzi, visit ABDO Publishing Company online. Web sites about Tony DiTerlizzi are featured on our Book Links page. These links are routinely monitored and updated to provide the most current information available.
www.abdopublishing.com

INDEX